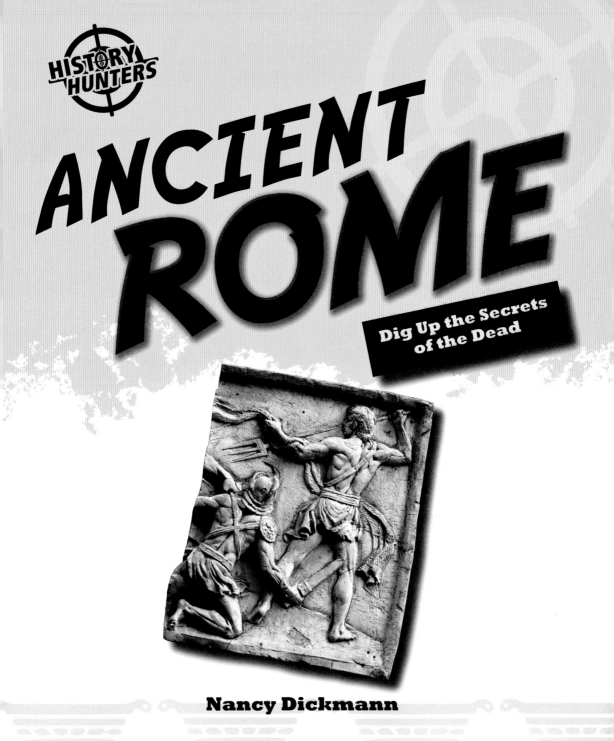

HISTORY HUNTERS

ANCIENT ROME

Nancy Dickmann

CAPSTONE PRESS
a capstone imprint

Produced for Capstone by Calcium
Edited by Sarah Eason and Jennifer Sanderson
Designed by Paul Myerscough
Picture research by Rachel Blount
Consultant: John Malam
Production by Paul Myerscough
Originated by Calcium Creative Limited © 2016
Printed and bound in China

20 19 18 17 16
10 9 8 7 6 5 4 3 2 1

Library of Congress Cataloging-in-Publication Data
Hardback ISBN 978 1 5157 2550 3
e-book ISBN 978 1 5157 2556 5

Acknowledgments
The author and publisher are grateful to the following for permission to reproduce copyright material: Getty
Images p. 20 (DEA/A. DAGLI ORTI); Shutterstock cover (Oleg Senkov), pp. 1 (Clara), 4 (Viacheslav Lopatin),
5 (Oleg Senkov), 6 (John Lumb), 9 (Regien Paassen), 12 (PLRANG ART), 14 (Galushko Sergey), 19 (Allou),
26 (Clara), 28 (Pavel Ilyukhin), 29 (Andrey Lebedev); Wellcome Images pp. 23 (Science Museum, London), 25
(Science Museum, London); Wikimedia Commons pp. 7 (Arpingstone), 8 (Notafly), 10 (Livioandronico2013), 11
(Gun Powder Ma), 13 (Fabien Dany), 15 (Luis García (Zaqarbal), 16 (Sailko), 17 (MatthiasKabel), 18 (Sailko),
21 (Arnoldius), 22 (Michael F. Mehnert), 24 (Twdk), 27 (Carole Raddato).

CONTENTS

Throughout the book you will find Deadly Secrets boxes that show an historical object. Use the clues and the hint in these boxes to figure out what the object is or what it was used for. Then check out the Answer box at the bottom of the page to see if you are right.

ANCIENT ROME

Around 2,000 years ago, a mighty **empire** stretched from one end of the Mediterranean Sea to the other. From its base in Rome, Italy, this empire reached as far as Britain in the north, Spain in the west, Iraq and the Black Sea in the east, and the lands of North Africa.

People have been living on the banks of the Tiber River, in what is now Italy, for more than 3,000 years. The earliest people who lived there were the Latins. They were farmers and herders who lived in villages. Eventually, about 2,800 years ago, these villages merged to form a single town named Rome.

The Romans left behind buildings such as the Colosseum, which can still be visited today.

From Republic to Empire

Neighboring peoples in Italy, such as the Etruscans to the north and the Sabines to the south, influenced Roman culture. Etruscan kings ruled Rome for a while. The kings were disliked by the Roman people. In 509 BCE, they were overthrown and the Roman **Republic** was born. Using a mixture of military power and political agreements, the Romans took over more and more of the land that is now Italy. From its modest beginnings, Rome grew into a great city. Rome's traders brought goods, such as pottery, wine, and spices, from distant lands. They also brought new ideas about science, literature, and art. By 27 BCE, the Republic became an empire, ruled by an **emperor**. It became the most powerful empire in the world.

Secrets of the Dead

Romulus and Remus

Roman historians told this story about the founding of their city: long ago, twin boys, named Romulus and Remus, were born. Their father was rumored to be Mars, the god of war. Their uncle thought that they might be a threat to his power so he ordered them to be drowned in the Tiber. However, the boys drifted ashore. They were found by a female wolf. The wolf fed the boys and soon, a kind shepherd took them in. Later, they returned as men. They killed their uncle and fought over who should rule the new city. In their quarrel, Romulus killed Remus. He named the city Rome, after himself.

Romulus and Remus became an important symbol for the Romans. This statue shows them as infants, feeding from a female wolf.

DIGGING UP THE PAST

The Romans left behind buildings, roads, bridges, and other structures that can still be seen today. These remains tell only part of the story. Without the hard work of **archaeologists** over many years, we would know much less about the daily lives of ordinary Romans.

Roman **artifacts** have been found across a huge area. This area covers most of western and central Europe as well as North Africa and western Asia. The Romans traded with distant cultures so sometimes artifacts can be found farther away.

DEADly Secrets

In CE 79, the Roman city of Pompeii was completely buried by ash after the eruption of Vesuvius, a nearby volcano. About 250 years ago, archaeologists started to dig out the city. They found a huge number of things that had been preserved by the ash, including this one. What do you think it is?

Hint: It is not a statue.

These archaeologists are still finding more historical artifacts near the **Forum** in Rome.

Telling a Story

Archaeologists have found a huge range of items, from pots and tools to jewelry, wall paintings, and **mosaics**, showing scenes of daily life. They have also found letters, diaries, and graffiti on walls. Analyzing the bones of Roman skeletons gives us clues about what people ate. They also tell us what diseases they suffered from. Most of these artifacts were found buried but some come from shipwrecks.

Secrets of the Dead

Roman Writers

Writing in the Latin language, Roman writers produced plays and poetry. They also wrote about history, nature, science, and law. It seems amazing that books written 2,000 years ago still survive today. This is because even after the end of the Roman Empire, in the CE 400s, Christian **monks** carefully copied the writings. Thanks to the work of these monks, people can still enjoy the writing of Roman authors.

Answer: It is a cast of a human body. During the eruption, about 2,000 people were killed. Their bodies were covered with ash. Over the years, these bodies slowly decayed, leaving hollow spaces where the bodies had been. Archaeologists filled some spaces with plaster of Paris, which hardened to create the casts.

RICH RULERS AND UNBEATABLE SOLDIERS

In its early days, Rome was a republic. The Senate ruled Rome. It was made up of 300 rich men. Each year, two **consuls** were elected to oversee the government. In 45 BCE, a former consul named Julius Caesar seized power. He made himself the **dictator** of Rome. He was murdered the following year. In 27 BCE, Augustus became the first Roman emperor. The Roman Empire had begun.

The Roman army took over and added lands to the empire. When a new area was conquered, its people were often allowed to continue to follow their own customs. Those who fought back were killed or sold as **slaves**. Adding new lands made the Romans rich. However, the Roman Empire became so big that it was hard to control.

This model shows Rome as it would have been in the fourth century CE. The important public buildings are clustered in an area called the Forum.

In the Army

The first Roman army was made up of ordinary land-owning citizens, who were called on when needed. They had to bring their own weapons. They were not paid and they stayed only until the fighting finished. Later, the army became a full-time force. These professional soldiers were well trained. To many people, they seemed unbeatable.

The Roman army used technology to help it win battles. The army built huge catapults to launch rocks over city walls. It used **battering rams** to knock down the walls. Soldiers would advance in a closely packed formation called a "testudo." The soldiers in the testudo used their shields to make a solid barrier over their heads and around the edges.

"Testudo" is the Latin word for "tortoise." The formation was called that because it resembled a tortoise's protective shell.

Secrets of the Dead

Testing a Soldier's Strength

You had to be strong to be a Roman foot soldier. Could you carry all of this equipment?

- Metal helmet and armor
- Short sword
- Two throwing spears
- Dagger
- Shield
- Leather boots studded with hobnails (short heavy-headed nails)
- Cloak
- Spare clothes
- Food and water
- Cooking pot
- Spade
- Portable mill (used to grind corn)
- Two long wooden stakes (for building a protective fence)

STRAIGHT ROADS AND WIDESPREAD TRADE

The Roman Empire was enormous and well organized. The land was divided into provinces. Roads were built to link the provinces. The main roads eventually led to the city of Rome itself. Some roads today follow the same straight routes as the Roman roads.

Messengers on horseback used the roads to carry information between the **governors** of the provinces and the rulers in Rome. There were places along main roads where messengers found fresh horses. Messages could be taken as far as 149 miles (240 kilometers) in a day.

Across Europe, many Roman roads have survived. This one is in Rome itself.

The Port of Ostia

Rome was an important city. In the CE 100s, it had a population of around 1 million. However, it does not have a harbor. It is found on the Tiber River, about 15.5 miles (25 km) from the coast. Most ships were too big to sail up the river to Rome so they docked at the port of Ostia. From there, cargo was loaded onto barges and taken to Rome. The port was full of warehouses packed with goods from all over the world.

Merchant ships like these would have docked at the port of Ostia.

Getting Around

In the beginning, only the army used the roads. Later, ordinary people were able to use them. Traders carried their goods from one town to the next. Wealthy people used them to go on trips. Most Romans traveled on foot or in a horse-drawn carriage. Merchants often found it cheaper and easier to ship goods by boat. These boats sailed along rivers as well as across the Mediterranean Sea.

Archaeologists have found artifacts from all corners of the empire in Rome. By analyzing the materials or the craftsmanship, they can tell where they were made. For example, **amber** from the Baltic coast, far to the north, has been found. Trade went both ways: Roman glass bottles were found in a grave in Ethiopia in 2015.

KNOWING YOUR PLACE

In Roman times there was one thing every person wanted to be: a Roman citizen. This status came with rights and privileges. Citizens were treated better under the law. Male citizens could vote in elections, and many served in the army or in the government.

Being a citizen gave you rights. However, it did not necessarily mean that you were rich or powerful. Some citizens were rich, but most were ordinary farmers, storekeepers, or craftsmen. In the early days, all you needed to be a citizen was to have been born in Rome to parents who were citizens. Later, citizenship was extended to people from other parts of the empire.

Types of Citizens

Citizens were divided into two groups: patricians and plebeians. The patricians were members of rich, powerful families. They could trace back their history a long way. Everyone else was a plebeian. Some plebeians were extremely poor. Others, such as bankers or traders, were much richer and more successful.

The most important roles in the government were filled by men from patrician families.

Non-Citizens

If you lived outside Rome itself but within Roman territory, you were considered to be a "provincial." These people did not have as many rights as citizens. However, they had their freedom. They were much luckier than the bottom rung of Roman society: the slaves. Slavery was extremely common in ancient Rome. Masters owned slaves and in the early days, the slaves had no rights at all.

A rich woman, such as the one shown here, would have slaves to help her dress and arrange her hair.

Secrets of the Dead

Roman Slavery: the Facts

- Many people became slaves when they were captured during wars (they were prisoners of war).
- Criminals were made to work as slaves.
- Unskilled slaves worked as household servants, in mines, on farms, or doing other manual labor.
- Educated slaves could work as teachers, accountants, or doctors.
- Owners could free their slaves or slaves could save up to buy their freedom.
- A freed slave could become a Roman citizen.

ROMAN GODS
AND RELIGIOUS FESTIVALS

The Romans worshiped many different gods and goddesses. Some of these, such as Jupiter and Minerva, were believed to be extremely powerful. Stories and legends were told about them. They were worshiped in grand **temples**.

Different gods and goddesses controlled different aspects of life. For example, Mars was the god of war. Venus was the goddess of love. Many Roman gods were based on Greek gods. For example, Minerva, the goddess of wisdom, was the Roman equivalent of the Greek goddess Athena.

Neptune was the powerful god of the sea. Sailors offered prayers and sacrifices to him in order to travel safely.

14

Festivals and Shrines

The Romans believed that gods and goddesses should be honored with beautiful temples and **shrines**. They also thought that making offerings to the gods would ensure their protection. Religious festivals to honor the gods took place throughout the year.

Household Gods

Groups of household spirits called the "lares" and "penates" helped guard homes and neighborhoods. The Romans believed that praying to these gods and keeping them happy could ensure that their families would stay safe and healthy. Most homes had a small shrine, called a "lararium." There, offerings could be left for the lares and penates.

Secrets of the Dead

How the Romans Made a Sacrifice

- Romans chose something to honor the gods. Food, wine, and flowers were good but statues were better. Offering a valuable animal showed how much people really cared.
- Care was taken to choose the right animal. Cows were sacrificed to Jupiter. Rams were offered to Janus.
- The animal's head was sprinkled with wine and bread before its throat was cut.
- The animal's internal organs (such as the liver) were removed and inspected. Romans believed that this could help predict the future.
- The organs were burned and the meat served as part of a feast.

Answer: It is a statue of a "lar," or household god. It was found in Spain.

FAMILY LIFE
AND DIFFICULT CHILDHOODS

Families were important in Roman times. The father was known as a "paterfamilias." He was the head of the family. Everyone else, including the family's slaves, had to follow his orders.

DEADly Secrets

Most freeborn Roman boys would have worn an object similar to this. Many would be made of cheaper materials, such as leather or **bronze**. This one is made of gold so we know that it belonged to a boy from a wealthy family. What do you think it is?

Hint: Romans believed this would ward off evil spirits and keep the wearer safe. ....

Without modern medicine, having children was riskier in ancient Rome than it is now. Many women died in childbirth. Children often died in the first few years of life. Families relied on prayers, offerings, and lucky charms to keep their children safe and healthy.

Growing Up

Children from poor families, and those who were slaves, often had to work from an early age. Boys would often work alongside their fathers, learning their trade. Other children were luckier. They were well looked after. Children had simple toys to play with until they were old enough to go to school. Many girls did not go to school at all. Instead, their mothers taught them how to cook, clean, sew, and run a household. Girls would be married as young as the age of 12, although their husbands were often much older.

Secrets of the Dead

Roman Schools: the Facts

Who could go?	Boys and girls from rich families
What ages?	From 7 to 11. Boys could go to high school after that but girls could not
Class size?	About 12 pupils was the maximum
Time?	From sunrise until midday, with no breaks allowed
Subjects?	Reading and writing (Latin and Greek), history, and simple mathematics using an **abacus**

Children and adults enjoyed playing games that used the ankle bones of a sheep in a similar way to dice or jacks.

Answer: It is a "bulla." It is an **amulet** given to a freeborn boy when he was eight days old. On his sixteenth birthday, the boy would stop wearing his bulla. At 16, he was considered a man.

TOWN HOUSES AND COUNTRY VILLAS

The remains of many Roman homes have survived to the present day. They tell us how the Romans lived. Homes could be simple apartments or farmhouses for poorer people, or more luxurious residences for the rich.

In Ostia and Rome, the town house of a rich Roman family was called a "domus." It was arranged around a courtyard called an atrium. The kitchens, study, and dining room opened off the atrium. Bedrooms were on the first floor. There might have been a walled garden at the back.

High Rise Life

Many poor people lived in apartment blocks called "insulae." These could be up to seven stories high. There were often stores on the ground floor. Insulae could be crowded and dirty. Sometimes, they collapsed or caught fire.

The remains of rich people's town houses in the city of Ephesus (in modern-day Turkey) can still be seen today.

Originally, a floor would have been laid over these stacks of bricks, creating an open space beneath. The space was connected to a furnace in the basement. What do you think it was for?

Hint: They were used in **bathhouses** as well as in homes when the weather turned cold. • • • • • • • • • • • •

In the Country

Wealthy Romans often had a country estate. This was made up of a large house, called a **villa**, and the farmland that surrounded it. Slaves were used to work the fields. There were also tens of thousands of working farms, which were also called villas.

Secrets of the Dead

Roman Towns

A typical Roman town would be laid out in a grid pattern. There was a central square called the Forum. Temples and official buildings surrounded the Forum. Stores lined the streets. There would be markets for selling all types of goods—even slaves. Towns had **aqueducts** to bring fresh running water from the hills. They also had sewers beneath the streets, which took away waste. Most people had no running water at home, so public washrooms, bathhouses, and drinking fountains were important places.

Answer: It was part of a heating system called a hypocaust. Warm air from the furnace traveled through the spaces around the stacks, heating the house from the floor upward.

FOOD LOVERS AND WINE DRINKERS

The Romans loved food. Those who could afford it ate exotic food at elaborate dinner parties. Many Roman writings about food have survived. Some give recipes or information on farming. Others describe dinner parties.

For the poor, food was often plain. Meat was expensive so their diet would be mainly bread, porridge, and vegetable stew. People living in insulae were not allowed to light fires, in case the whole building caught alight. Instead, they bought cooked food from stores and street stalls. There were no refrigerators in Roman times, so food had to be salted or smoked to preserve it. Salted pork was a common meat. A salty fish sauce, called "garum," was a popular condiment added to food.

Romans would recline, or lie down, on a couch to eat. Rich people had slaves to serve them.

A Richer Diet

Wealthier Romans ate a simple breakfast of bread with eggs, cheese, or dried fruit. Lunch would consist of similar foods as well as meat or fish and vegetables, but it was still a small meal. Dinner was the main meal of the day. Sometimes, it included exotic food, such as ostrich meat. Spices were shipped in from across the empire to flavor food. The Romans drank a lot of wine, although they usually mixed it with water. It was also often mixed with spices or sweetened with honey.

These bronze sieves and dippers were found in Germany. They may have been used for straining spices and sediment out of wine.

Secrets of the Dead

Roman Dinner Party Etiquette

- DO recline on a couch to eat, on your left side propped up on your elbow. Only slaves and children sit on chairs to eat!
- DO make sure a slave washes your hands because you will be eating with your fingers.
- DO NOT fall asleep, even if the party goes on for hours and hours.
- DO burp loudly to show that you are enjoying the meal.
- DO NOT worry if you feel full. You are allowed to excuse yourself and make yourself sick in a side room, then come back and eat more.

ILLNESSES AND HERBAL MEDICINES

Life could be dangerous in Roman times. People often died of disease or injuries that would be easily treatable today, with modern medicine and technology. The Romans relied on a mixture of superstition and science to stay healthy.

Back then, no one knew that germs cause disease. Instead, many people blamed evil spirits if they were sick. Others thought that illness was a sign that the gods were punishing them. They dealt with health problems by praying and making offerings to the gods. Many people prayed to Asclepius.

In mythology, Asclepius was the god of medicine. He was an ancient Greek god whom the Romans adopted.

Doctors

Roman doctors tried to treat illness with science. Many of their ideas came from the ancient Greeks, and they brought Greek doctors to Rome. At first, only wealthy people could afford to see a doctor. Later, the government helped to pay for poor people to use them, too.

Doctors often used herbs to treat illnesses. For example, mustard seeds were used to treat snakebites, and lemon balm was used for headaches. Herbs could be ground up to make them into pills or ointments. More serious illnesses and injuries could be treated with surgery, although this was painful and could be fatal.

DEADly Secrets

This small model of a thumb is made of clay. An ordinary Roman left it at a religious building. What do you think it is for, and why would a person leave one at a temple?

Hint: It could either be used to ask for help or to give thanks. •••••

Secrets of the Dead

What a Surgeon Could Do for You:

- Remove a goiter (a type of swollen growth) from the neck
- Perform a Caesarean section to deliver a baby (although the mother always died)
- Repair a hernia
- Perform trepanation (drilling a hole through the skull to relieve pressure)
- Remove cataracts from the eyes to improve vision
- Amputation (cutting off) of injured arms or legs

Answer: This model was left as an offering to Asclepius or other gods. The shape of the object showed the body part that needed healing; in this case, a thumb.

LOOKING GOOD AND KEEPING CLEAN

For most ordinary Romans, the basic article of clothing was a simple short-sleeved **tunic** tied with a belt. However, wealthy Romans often used fashion as a way of showing off.

Men who were citizens sometimes wore a toga over their tunic. This large woolen cloth was wrapped carefully around the body. It was uncomfortable in hot weather but it was a way of showing your social status (how important and wealthy you were). Different colors meant different things. For example, political candidates wore white togas to show that they were honest.

Women's Clothes

Most women wore a long robe called a "stola." Over that, they would wear a shawl called a "palla." They draped the palla around their shoulders or put it over the head like a hood. The richest women would show off in expensive clothes made of silk or cotton from Asia.

A rich woman would have needed help to arrange her hair in this fashionable style.

Hair and Beauty

The Romans did not use soap. Instead, they rubbed scented oil onto their skin at the bathhouse. They scraped it off, along with the dirt. Roman men often went to the barber for a shave. Women's hair could be styled in a simple bun or pinned up in arrangements of curls, depending on the fashion of the time. It was fashionable to have pale skin. Pale skin meant that you were rich enough not to have to work outside in the Sun.

DEADly Secrets

This curved bronze instrument would have been used at a bathhouse. Can you guess what it was for?

Hint: It was used with bath oils. •••••••••••••••

Secrets of the Dead

Public Bathing

Public bathhouses were an important part of Roman city life. They were a place to get clean, relax, and gossip. Men and women went to the baths at separate times. Some of a bathhouse's main rooms included:

- Changing rooms
- A massage room
- A hot, steamy room like a sauna
- A hot pool for washing
- A lukewarm pool for cooling down
- A cold, open-air swimming pool
- An exercise yard called a "palestra"
- **Communal** toilets

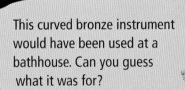

Answer: This is a "strigil." The curved end was used for scraping off the oil that Romans used at a bathhouse. Wealthy Romans would bring a slave to do the scraping for them.

GRUESOME GAMES AND DRAMATIC PLAYS

There was no shortage of ways for Romans to spend their free time. Gossiping with friends in the bathhouse was just one option. Romans could also watch plays and chariot racing and fighting contests, which were known simply as games.

Emperors and other important men staged the games as a way of winning popularity with the public. These contests were cruel and bloody. Trained fighters called **gladiators** sometimes fought to the death. There were different types of gladiators, and each used different weapons and fighting styles.

Beasts and Chariots

The games also featured wild animals, either being hunted or tearing people apart. Sometimes, battles were **reenacted**. Chariot racing was dangerous. It was very popular. The biggest racetrack in Rome could seat 250,000 people. The competitors drove lightweight chariots pulled by as many as eight horses. The track had tight turns that often resulted in spectacular crashes.

Gladiators such as these were often slaves, prisoners of war, or criminals. They were forced to fight.

Roman Theater

The Romans watched plays in large outdoor **amphitheaters**. Drama was popular and at first, mostly Greek plays were performed. Later, Roman playwrights, such as Plautus, wrote their own plays. The actors often wore masks to show emotion. Only men were allowed to be actors, so they played the female parts, too.

DEADly Secrets

Soldiers in the army did not wear helmets like this one. Look at its features. Can you tell who would have worn it?

Hint: He was a kind of gladiator. • • • • • • • • •

Secrets of the Dead

A Guide to Gladiator Spotting

- Thracian: wears a helmet with a wide brim and carries a small shield and a short, curved sword
- Samnite: wears a helmet and carries a long rectangular shield and a short sword
- Retiarius: fights with a trident (like a pitchfork), a dagger, and a net
- Murmillo: wears a helmet with a crest
- Dimachaerus: uses two swords, one in each hand

Answer: This bronze helmet is of the style often worn by a "murmillo" fighter. He would have been armed with a sword and a shield, with thick padding or armor to protect his sword arm.

AMAZING ENGINEERING

The Romans were incredible **engineers**. They were able to build structures that were bigger, stronger, and longer-lasting than those of many other **civilizations**.

They also built systems of roads and sewers, heating systems, and aqueducts that were necessary to keep the empire running.

Secrets of the Dead

Pantheon Facts

- The enormous dome is 142 feet (43.3 m) across.
- There are no windows except for the oculus (hole) in the center of the dome. It is 25.6 feet (7.8 m) across.
- The concrete of the dome ranges from 3.9 feet (1.2 m) thick near the oculus to 21 feet (6.4 m) thick at the base.
- The columns supporting the portico (porch) were brought all the way from Egypt. They weigh 60 tons (54.4 mt) each.

The Pantheon in Rome was built in about CE 120. It was a temple to all the gods.

Strong and Beautiful

In the second century BCE, Roman engineers mixed volcanic ash with lime, crushed brick and tile, and water to make a new substance called concrete. Concrete is light and strong. It can be molded into any shape. It allowed the Romans to build structures that were tall and strong enough not to collapse under their own weight.

Roman buildings were also beautiful. Shapes such as arches allowed engineers to design big, airy rooms. Grand public buildings could be clad, or covered, in stone or polished marble. Houses and other buildings were often painted bright colors and decorated with beautiful frescoes (wall paintings) and mosaics.

Massive aqueducts like this one in Segovia, Spain, brought fresh water from the hills into Roman towns and cities.

Built to Last

Much of what the Romans built is still standing today. It allows archaeologists to learn a huge amount about their engineering abilities and about how they built their society. Smaller artifacts such as letters, jewelry, and offerings to gods show us what life was like for individual people. Archaeologists are still making new discoveries, allowing us to learn even more about this fascinating civilization.

GLOSSARY

abacus device with beads on rods that is used for counting and calculations

amber hard, yellow or brown material that comes from the sap of pine trees. It is cut and polished to make jewelry

amphitheater outdoor theater

amulet small item worn for good luck or to ward off evil

aqueduct pipe or channel for carrying water

archaeologist person who digs up and studies the remains of ancient cultures

artifact object made by a human being that has cultural or religious importance

bathhouse public building where people can go to exercise and get clean

battering ram large beam used to break down walls or doors, or to make a hole in the side of a ship

bronze metal made from a mixture of copper and tin

civilization society, culture, and way of life of a particular area

communal shared

consul most high-ranking government official in ancient Rome

dictator person who rules a country with total authority and often in a cruel or brutal way

emperor ruler of an empire

empire collection of territories ruled by an emperor

engineer person whose job is designing buildings or other structures

Forum open space in the center of a town or city, where government buildings were located

gladiator someone who was trained to fight as a way of providing entertainment for people

governor official who ruled a region

monk man who has joined a religious community and promised to live a simple life

mosaic picture made from many small pieces of colored stone or glass

reenact act out something that took place earlier

republic country whose rulers are elected by the people

shrine sacred place devoted to honoring a god

slave person who is owned by someone else and forced to work without pay

temple building where gods and goddesses are worshiped

tunic simple garment made from two rectangles of cloth stitched together and tied with a belt

villa large house in the countryside, often surrounded by fields and farms

READ MORE

Books

Catel, Patrick. *What Did the Ancient Romans Do for Me?* (Linking the Past and Present). North Mankato, MN: Heinemann, 2011.

James, Simon. *Ancient Rome* (DK Eyewitness Books). New York: Dorling Kindersley, 2015.

Klar, Jeremy. *The Totally Gross History of Ancient Rome* (Totally Gross History). New York: Rosen Central, 2016.

O'Shei, Tim. *Secrets of Pompeii: Buried City of Ancient Rome* (Archaeological Mysteries). North Mankato, MN: Capstone, 2015.

Waldron, Melanie. *Geography Matters in Ancient Rome* (Geography Matters in Ancient Civilizations). North Mankato, MN: Heinemann, 2015.

Web Sites

Explore life in ancient Rome using this interactive map:
www.dkfindout.com/us/history/ancient-rome

Learn about ancient Roman language, myths, and more:
http://education.nationalgeographic.org/ancient-rome/?ar_a=1

This web site has information about daily life in ancient Rome, including schools, food, houses, and slavery:
http://quatr.us/romans/people

Find out more about Roman buildings:
www.roman-empire.net/children/builders.html

INDEX